C000136950

Photo by Susan Cook

Justin Deas, Ted Marcoux and Jennifer Van Dyck in a scene from the Second Stage

EARTH AND SKY

A Poetic Thriller for the Stage

BY DOUGLAS POST

★

★

DRAMATISTS
PLAY SERVICE
INC.

© Copyright, 1991, by Douglas Post
© Copyright, 1987, by Douglas Post
as an unpublished dramatic composition

CAUTION: Professionals and amateurs are hereby warned that EARTH AND SKY is subject to a royalty. It is fully protected under the copyright laws of the United States of America, and of all countries covered by the International Copyright Union (including the Dominion of Canada and the rest of the British Commonwealth), and of all countries covered by the Pan-American Copyright Convention and the Universal Copyright Convention, and of all countries with which the United States has reciprocal copyright relations. All rights, including professional, amateur, motion picture, recitation, lecturing, public reading, radio broadcasting, television, video or sound taping, all other forms of mechanical or electronic reproduction, such as information storage and retrieval systems and photocopying, and the rights of translation into foreign languages, are strictly reserved. Particular emphasis is laid upon the question of readings, permission for which must be secured from the author's agent in writing.

The stage performance rights in EARTH AND SKY (other than first class rights) are controlled exclusively by the DRAMATISTS PLAY SERVICE, INC., 440 Park Avenue South, New York, N.Y. 10016. No professional or non-professional performance of the play (excluding first class professional performance) may be given without obtaining in advance the written permission of the DRAMATISTS PLAY SERVICE, INC., and paying the requisite fee.

Inquiries concerning all other rights should be addressed to The Tantleff Office, 375 Greenwich Street, Suite 700, New York, N.Y. 10013.

SPECIAL NOTE

All groups receiving permission to produce EARTH AND SKY are required (1) to give credit to the author as sole and exclusive author of the play in all programs distributed in connection with performances of the play and in all instances in which the title of the play appears for purposes of advertising, publicizing or otherwise exploiting the play, and/or a production thereof; the name of the author must appear on a separate line, in which no other name appears, immediately beneath the title and in size and prominence of type equal to 50% of the largest, most prominent letter used for the title of the play. No person, firm or entity may receive credit larger or more prominent than that accorded the Author, and (2) to give the following acknowledgment in all programs distributed in connection with performances of the play:

EARTH AND SKY was originally produced as a staged reading at the 1989 National Playwrights Conference at the Eugene O'Neill Theatre Center.

Original New York Production by
Second Stage Theatre on January 17, 1991.

"This Side of the Truth" and "They Are The Only Dead Who Did Not Love"
by Dylan Thomas are used with permission of
the Trustees for Copyrights of Dylan Thomas.

SOUND EFFECTS

The following is a list of sound effects referenced in thisplay:
Police siren
Subway train
Traffic
Telephone ring
Birds chirping
Ocean

*"What is it that makes someone a link
between you and your own life?"*

— *Maria Irene Fornes*

*"The white moonlight was cold and clear,
like the justice we dream of but don't find."*

— *Raymond Chandler*

This play is dedicated to Nancy

EARTH AND SKY was first produced at the Second Stage Theatre (Robyn Goodman and Carole Rothman, Artistic Directors) in New York City on February 4, 1991. It was directed by Andre Ernotte; the set design was by William Barclay; the costume design was by Deborah Shaw; the lighting design was by Phil Monat; the sound design was by Bruce Ellman; the production stage manager was Crystal Huntington; and the stage manager was J. Courtney Pollard. The cast was as follows:

SARA MCKEON .... Jennifer Van Dyck
DAVID AMES .... Ted Marcoux
DETECTIVE AL KERSNOWSKI .... Ron Nakahara
DETECTIVE H.E. WEBER .... Justin Deas
JOYCE LAZLO .... Lisa Arrindell
BILLY HART .... Michael Genet
CARL EISENSTADT .... Evan Thompson
MARIE DEFARIA .... Lisa Beth Miller
JULIUS GATZ .... Paul Kandel

EARTH AND SKY was originally presented as a staged reading at the 1989 National Playwrights Conference at the Eugene O'Neill Theater Center in Waterford, Connecticut, on July 20, 1989. It was directed by Margaret Booker; the set design was by G.W. Mercer; the lighting design was by Tina Charney. The cast was as follows:

SARA MCKEON .... Kate Burton
DAVID AMES .... Kevin Geer
DETECTIVE AL KERSNOWSKI .... Paul McCrane
DETECTIVE H.E. WEBER .... Earl Hindman
JOYCE LAZLO .... Gabrielle Carteris
BILLY HART .... Michael Genet
CARL EISENSTADT .... John Seitz
MARIE DEFARIA .... Jane Kaczmarek
JULIUS GATZ .... Christopher Centrella

EARTH AND SKY was the winner of the 1990 L. Arnold Weissberger Award sponsored by New Dramatists.

CHARACTERS

SARA MCKEON, late 20s
DAVID AMES, early 30s
DETECTIVE AL KERSNOWSKI, mid 30s
DETECTIVE H.E. WEBER, 40
JOYCE LAZLO, early 20s
BILLY HART, early 30s
CARL EISENSTADT, 50
MARIE DEFARIA, early 30s
JULIUS GATZ, 40

TIME

August of the present year.

PLACE

The city of Chicago.

EARTH AND SKY should be performed without an intermission.

EARTH AND SKY

Scene 1

The setting of this play is theatrical as opposed to real. A grid-like structure that can be utilized to suggest a variety of locations. Gritty, urban and underground. Real furniture and props should be kept to an absolute minimum. The shifts in locale should happen through lighting and sound and the words that the characters speak. The action is fluid. One scene bleeds right into the next. At the moment Sara and David stand at opposite ends of the stage. They are in the midst of a telephone conversation. Kersnowski sits between them sipping coffee from a Styrofoam cup.

DAVID. Sara?

SARA. Hi.

DAVID. Did I wake you?

SARA. No. It's alright. I was just starting to drift off.

DAVID. Sorry, it's so late.

SARA. What time is it?

DAVID. Twelve. Twelve-thirty. I would have called sooner, but it's been merry hell around here.

SARA. You're still at work?

DAVID. Oh, yeah.

SARA. So it's been busy?

DAVID. You could say that.

SARA. And how did it go with the conventioneers?

DAVID. They trashed the place. Complained about the food, finished off my liquor supply, and left a two dollar tip. *(Pause.)* How are *you*?

SARA. I'm fine. I'm ... real good.

DAVID. Yeah?

SARA. Yeah.

DAVID. That's good. (P*ause.*) Again. The hour. I —

SARA. It's okay. Really. I was only halfway into a dream.

DAVID. Oh.

SARA. That night out on the rocks. In the park. When you first approached me. I was so frightened. Remember?

DAVID. Sure.

SARA. I was dreaming about that. *(Pause.)* Remember how we stood there for the longest time? Just watching the water come in? Listening to the sound of the waves?

DAVID. I do.

SARA. And the walk we took afterwards? Me, babbling incoherently. You, pretending to understand every word.

DAVID. Hey, I was captivated.

SARA. And then coming home. Here. To the apartment. God, the awkwardness. I didn't want you to think I was ... you know.

DAVID. Easy?

SARA. Yes.

DAVID. Believe me. I would never think that of you. *(She laughs.)*

SARA. Do you remember what you said that night?

DAVID. I said a lot of things.

SARA. About why it is that people fall in love?

DAVID. Oh, yeah. I sounded like a fortune cookie.

SARA. From scratch, you said. Everything could open up. Everything could start again. I'll never forget. *(Pause.)* I never will. *(Pause.)* Hurry up and come home, okay?

DAVID. Sara —

SARA. What?

DAVID. I — *(Pause.)* I can't be there tonight. *(Pause.)*

SARA. What's wrong?

DAVID. I just got a call. Someone I used to know. A woman I ... used to go out with. She ... *(Pause.)* She tried to kill herself. *(Pause.)*

SARA. Oh, God.

DAVID. Tried to cut her wrists open. I mean, she did. She cut her ... both of her wrists. Open. Somebody found her. Took her to emergency. Anyway. She's home.

SARA. She ... called you?

DAVID. Just now. A few minutes ago. She wants to see me. I have to go.

SARA. Of course.

DAVID. I don't know how long this'll take. When I'll, you know ... be through.

SARA. No. Just go.

DAVID. I'll come by. Whenever I get done. I'll be there. But don't wait up for me. Please. Go back to bed.

SARA. Alright.

DAVID. Sara? *(Pause.)* Sara, I'm sorry this had to happen.

SARA. It's alright. You should ... go.

DAVID. I will. I will. I ... *(Pause.)* I better hang up.

SARA. Okay. *(He does. A moment. Then she hangs up.)*

Scene 2

Sara moves to another part of the stage where she changes from the man's shirt she is wearing into a summer dress. She will wear this dress for the remainder of the play. David also stays on stage. Weber enters and crosses to Kersnowski. Kersnowski rises. We are in an alley.

KERSNOWSKI. Morning.

WEBER. Yeah.

KERSNOWSKI. Sorry I had to —

WEBER. Don't apologize.

KERSNOWSKI. I mean, I woke the wife.

WEBER. You woke the wife. It's not exactly catastrophic. She falls back on the mattress and sleeps till noon. Me, I'm out of the house on an empty stomach wearing yesterday's socks. *(Pause.)*

KERSNOWSKI. Want a bagel?

WEBER. Not particularly. *(Pause.)* So what is the impetus for this assembly?

KERSNOWSKI. Pardon me?

WEBER. What am I doing here?

9

KERSNOWSKI. Oh. Body found in the bottom of the dumpster. Bullet in the back of the head.

WEBER. Sweet.

KERSNOWSKI. Yeah. Real pleasant.

WEBER. What else?

KERSNOWSKI. Uh ... that's it. That's all we know. *(Pause.)*

WEBER. That's it? Al, what do you suppose it is they're paying us for?

KERSNOWSKI. Beats me.

WEBER. Hazard a guess.

KERSNOWSKI. City service?

WEBER. Don't be a smart ass, okay?

KERSNOWSKI. Okay.

WEBER. Tell me things.

KERSNOWSKI. Like what?

WEBER. Man or woman?

KERSNOWSKI. Male Caucasian.

WEBER. Any ID?

KERSNOWSKI. Yes.

WEBER. Money in the wallet?

KERSNOWSKI. No.

WEBER. Witnesses?

KERSNOWSKI. Somebody heard a shot.

WEBER. What time?

KERSNOWSKI. They don't know.

WEBER. Perfect. *(Pause.)* Let me see the bagel. *(Kersnowski reaches into his pocket. He rummages. Weber looks at him.)* Never mind. *(Pause.)* This alley stinks. What is that?

KERSNOWSKI. The heat.

WEBER. The heat makes it smell so bad?

KERSNOWSKI. I think so. Yes.

WEBER. Where's the wallet?

KERSNOWSKI. Being examined.

WEBER. Very good. What's the vic's name?

KERSNOWSKI. Ames. David Ames.

WEBER. Ames?

KERSNOWSKI. Sounds familiar, don't it?

WEBER. David ... Ames. *(Pause.)*

KERSNOWSKI. Wait a minute.
WEBER. Yeah.
KERSNOWSKI. Wait a.... Aw, Christ.
WEBER. Uh-huh. *(Pause.)*
KERSNOWSKI. Lapointe.
WEBER. Good morning.

Scene 3

*The sound of a police siren. Weber and Kersnowski cross to
Sara. She turns to them. We are in Sara's apartment. David
remains onstage.*

WEBER. Miss McKeon?
SARA. Yes?
WEBER. Sara McKeon?
SARA. Yes.
WEBER. My name is Detective Weber. This is Detective
Kersnowski.
KERSNOWSKI. How do you do, ma'am?
WEBER. We're sorry to barge in on you this way, but uh ...
I'm afraid we have some rather disturbing news to bring you.
(Pause.) A friend of yours ... a Mr. David Ames was found dead
earlier today. *(Pause.)* He was, ah ... he was shot, Miss McKeon.
At very close range. From behind. His body was then placed
within a, ah ... a garbage dumpster. He was discovered there
this morning. We notified the next of kin. In this case, his
father. He came down and identified the body. And he told
us about you. *(Pause.)*
SARA. David ... ?
KERSNOWSKI. David Ames. Yes, ma'am. *(Pause.)*
SARA. Oh, Christ. Oh ... oh, my God.
KERSNOWSKI. Maybe you should sit down. *(She does.)*
SARA. I just ... *(She shakes her head.)* I spoke to him —
WEBER. When?
SARA. What?
WEBER. When did you speak to him? *(Pause. David leaves the*

11

stage.) Miss McKeon, we understand the state of shock you must be in. We really do. And we could go away now. But a few questions put to you at this time might make all the difference between finding this man's killer and letting this incident drop into a crack behind some fat policeman's desk. *(Pause.)* What I mean to say is, you could really help us out. *(Pause.)*

KERSNOWSKI. We should go.

SARA. No. *(Pause.)* No, I ... I'll try.

WEBER. Thank you, Miss McKeon. We'll make this quick. *(Weber lights up a cigarette. Kersnowski takes notes.)* You knew David Ames well? *(She nods.)* Intimately?

SARA. We ... we were lovers.

WEBER. I see. And had this involvement taken place over a long period of time?

SARA. Two and a half months.

WEBER. Uh-huh. And before that ...?

SARA. We met two and a half months ago. Oh, my God. They shot him in the head?

KERSNOWSKI. It would have been painless for him, ma'am. Almost instantaneous.

WEBER. During these two and a half months, Miss McKeon, you and Mr. Ames saw each other ... what? Often?

SARA. Everyday.

WEBER. Uh-huh. And your last conversation ...?

SARA. It was last night. He ... he called to tell me ... *(Pause.)*

WEBER. Called to tell you ... what?

SARA. That he couldn't be here. That something had ... had happened to a friend of his.

WEBER. A friend?

SARA. A woman. She'd made an attempt at suicide. She'd called him. He was going to meet her.

WEBER. Where?

SARA. He didn't say.

KERSNOWSKI. A suicide?

SARA. Yes. She'd ... cut her wrists open. But she was okay. He said.

KERSNOWSKI. What is this woman's name? Do you recall?

12

SARA. No. He didn't tell me.

WEBER. What time was this?

SARA. I ... I don't remember. Past midnight. Oh, Jesus.

KERSNOWSKI. We're almost done here, ma'am. Please, stay with us. *(She nods.)*

WEBER. Miss McKeon, your understanding of what David Ames did for a living ... what would that be?

SARA. He ... he owned a restaurant. It's called the Fast Track.

WEBER. Uh-huh. Were you aware of any ... independent ventures that he might have participated in?

SARA. Ventures?

WEBER. Away from the restaurant. Other sources of income, say. *(She shakes her head.)* Alright. When you and he weren't ... together ... in each other's company ... do you know where he went? What he did? *(She shakes her head again.)* Did you ever ask for an accounting of his whereabouts?

SARA. No.

WEBER. And he didn't volunteer the information.

KERSNOWSKI. H. E. —

SARA. Why are you asking me these questions?

KERSNOWSKI. H. E., maybe we should be —

WEBER. Right. Let me wrap this up. I have in my notes that you're a writer.

SARA. Yes.

WEBER. A poet. *(Pause.)*

SARA. Yes.

WEBER. A writer of poetry. *(Pause.)* And you work part-time. At the library. Downtown. *(Pause.)*

SARA. Yes.

WEBER. One more item, Miss McKeon. It's a question of character. A matter of judgement, really. Would you say that you knew David Ames ... well?

SARA. You have to leave now. *(Pause.)*

WEBER. Of course. We've imposed upon you far too much. You've been very helpful, Miss McKeon. If there's anything —

SARA. No. You have to leave. Now. *(Pause.)*

KERSNOWSKI. Thank you, ma'am. We're really very sorry. *(Kersnowski exits. Weber remains looking at Sara. A moment.)*

WEBER. My sincere regrets, Miss McKeon. *(He turns and exits. Silence. Sara holds herself. She looks away. She breathes deeply. Then it all comes out.)*
SARA. Oh, my God. Oh, Jesus. *(Pause.)* David?

Scene 4

Joyce enters carrying a stack of books. She is talking. Sara moves to another part of the stage and opens a book. We are in a library.

JOYCE. It's got to do with information. That's what I think. I mean, look at it this way. How can a society, a democratic society, be expected to function if there isn't that ... what? Freedom of information. One place to go and say: Yes. Here is the source of truth. That's what attracted me to the notion of the job in the first place. More so than, say, the social sciences or teaching or urban planning. Because, here, here you can see it all. Right there in front of you. Step out onto the street and what do you find? Blind men and simpletons. Here, there is knowledge. Outside ... what is it a friend of mine said? The celebration of ignorance. *(Pause.)* Do you see what I'm getting at?
SARA. I do.
JOYCE. That's what makes the work special.
SARA. Yes.
JOYCE. God, I'm rambling, I know. First day jitters. Um ... where should I put these?
SARA. Anywhere you like. It really doesn't matter. *(Joyce laughs.)*
JOYCE. Well, now, that's another sermon of mine. the concept of order. Who was it who said: "So quick bright things come to confusion?"
SARA. I'm sorry.
JOYCE. What?
SARA. You've already told me twice today. Your name.
JOYCE. Joyce.

SARA. Yes. Joyce. *(Pause.)* Joyce, do you suppose that you could just ... talk less?
JOYCE. Of course, I ... *(Pause.)* Yes. *(Joyce exits with the books. Sara turns a page. A moment. Joyce enters.)* I ... I'm so sorry. I didn't know. The guard just told me. I had no idea. I — *(Sara looks away.)* Sara, are you alright? *(She looks at Joyce. A moment.)*
SARA. No.

Scene 5

David enters as Joyce exits. We are in Sara's apartment.

DAVID. What's the matter?
SARA. God, you frightened me.
DAVID. Sorry. I didn't mean to. I just walked into the room and found you, you know ... standing that way. Staring into space. *(Pause.)* So what's up?
SARA. Nothing.
DAVID. Nothing? *(She shakes her head.)*
SARA. It's these grey days. They always bring it out in me. I've been reading about these airline disasters. These ... tragedies that have become an implicit part of our lives. I have a theory.
DAVID. Okay.
SARA. I think the pilots get depressed.
DAVID. Uh-huh.
SARA. No, really. It's become the thing to do. You're sort of ostracized if you're not seeing a therapist. Or taking lithium. Or receiving shock treatments. *(David laughs.)* You laugh, but depression has become a going concern. It's the new national pastime. I think these men feed right into it. They start to ruminate, way up there in the skies, about the state of things and how little they actually have to contribute against the force of nature. And before they know it they're headed into the side of some mountain and all the while thinking: "Oh, well. I'm just living out my function. Contributing to the collapse of western civilization and all that."

15

DAVID. The collapse of western civilization?

SARA. Yes.

DAVID. I thought we were talking about airplanes.

SARA. But it's all part of the same thing. If, in point of fact, you've accepted the idea that the organism is dying. That what we are actually doing is destroying ourselves. Willfully and with a purpose.

DAVID. Okay. Now comes my question. Is that what *you* believe?

SARA. No, of course not. I mean, I couldn't live that way.

DAVID. So?

SARA. So that doesn't mean I'm not susceptible to it. It's in the air these days. The climate. The ... the social fabric. Everything starts to wear you down. If you let it. Don't you find that to be the case?

DAVID. Um —

SARA. I mean, honestly, David, these are the questions. How do you go about sustaining yourself? What gets you out of bed in the morning?

DAVID. Well, speaking for myself, I would have to say: You. *(She laughs.)* No, I mean it. And not just in the physical sense. I mean it ... what's that word?

SARA. Figuratively?

DAVID. Yes. Figuratively. I wake up feeling good. I get through each day now, no problem, 'cause I know I'm coming back here at night to your apartment. And you're waiting for me. And you make me better than I am. You make me happy. Real, real happy. *(Pause.)* So maybe I should become a pilot. *(She laughs.)*

SARA. No. No, please. You're gone enough as it is. I want you here. With me. *(He goes to her. They kiss.)*

DAVID. Listen. About that.

SARA. About what?

DAVID. That thing we talked about. A few weeks ago. Going away. Getting out of town. Out of this hemisphere. *(Pause.)* I think we should do it.

SARA. Really?

DAVID. Absolutely. I've been looking into it. I could sell the place at a slight profit. I think. Plus. Plus, as I mentioned before, there's some money coming in.

SARA. We don't need it.

DAVID. I know, I know. But we'll have it anyway.

SARA. Where will we go?

DAVID. Mexico. Copenhagen. New Zealand. Who knows? We'll just go. We won't tell anyone. We'll just ... take off.

SARA. David, are you serious?

DAVID. I have never been more so. I want to get out of this hell hole. I want to go somewhere and start over.

SARA. When?

DAVID. The sooner, the better.

SARA. I ... I'd have to give notice.

DAVID. After I've finalized the deal.

SARA. Sublet the apartment.

DAVID. Shouldn't be tough.

SARA. Sell off my worldly possessions.

DAVID. Both of them? *(She laughs.)*

SARA. We're really going to do this, aren't we?

DAVID. If it's what you want. *(Pause.)*

SARA. Yes. Yes, it is absolutely what I want. *(She holds him. She starts to cry.)*

DAVID. Hey. Hey, are you alright? *(She laughs.)*

SARA. Yes. Yes, I ... God, my heart's going. I don't know why I ... what's going on?

DAVID. You're shaking.

SARA. I know, I —

DAVID. Are you okay?

SARA. Yes, I'm fine. I'm just ... surprised.

DAVID. Hey, maybe this is what happiness feels like.

SARA. Yes. Yes, maybe so.

DAVID. Get used to it. *(She laughs. They kiss again.)* I got to go.

SARA. So soon?

DAVID. 'Fraid so. I got some conventioneers coming in from the auto show. Guys let loose on the town one night out of the year looking for a little pandemonium. I'll call you when there's a break in the action.

17

SARA. I'll be here. *(He starts to go. He turns and looks at her. A moment.)* What?

DAVID. I was just thinking. I've known you for ten weeks. Ten weeks. To the day. *(She smiles.)*

SARA. A lifetime.

DAVID. Yeah. A lifetime. *(Pause.)* Still sad?

SARA. Nope.

DAVID. Under the weather?

SARA. Huh-uh.

DAVID. Depressed? *(She laughs.)*

SARA. How could I be? *(Pause.)* I mean, we're bailing out of the airplane. Right? *(They kiss again.)*

Scene 6

Weber enters as David exits. We are in the back room of his police station. Sara turns to Weber.

WEBER. Miss McKeon.

SARA. They told me out front I might find you back here. I hope you don't mind. I —

WEBER. No. Please. Sit down.

SARA. Thank you. *(She does.)*

WEBER. Well. You look ... much better than the last time I saw you. How are you holding up?

SARA. Alright. The last few days have been pretty terrible. But I'm starting to function again. I think.

WEBER. That's good to hear. Can I get you something?

SARA. No.

WEBER. Coffee around here tastes kind of like toilet water, but —

SARA. Nothing. Thank you. *(Pause.)* I hope I'm not keeping you from anything.

WEBER. Me? No. Well, my wife's unpaid parking tickets.

SARA. Oh. Are there a lot?

WEBER. Yes. I think she's trying to set some kind of record. *(Pause.)* I was going to telephone you, Miss McKeon. Or come

18

by at some point.

SARA. I just wanted to find out if you'd made any progress identifying David's killer.

WEBER. We got our man.

SARA. You ... you do?

WEBER. Or we know who we're looking for, at least.

SARA. Who?

WEBER. His name is Emilio Sanchez. He was a short-order cook at a little dive underneath the el tracks. Billy Hart's Bar and Grill. This is all of about thirty yards from the dumpster where we found the body. Seems that Sanchez hasn't shown up for the job this week. Owner says he disappeared the night of the killing. We checked the records on him. Turns out this guy got pulled in on a felony about eighteen months ago. We took his prints then. They match the set we found on the victim's wallet. *(Pause.)* And that, as they say, is pretty much that.

SARA. But you haven't arrested him?

WEBER. At this point his whereabouts are still unknown. But we got an APB out on him. We're talking to friends. Enemies. Anyone in the neighborhood. Something'll turn up. It always does.

SARA. Always?

WEBER. *Almost* always, Miss McKeon.

SARA. I see. *(Pause. Weber lights up a cigarette.)*

WEBER. You seem less than satisfied. This is supposed to be good news. What we in the trade refer to as a breakthrough.

SARA. I'm still not clear on how it happened. Or why.

WEBER. My guess is that Sanchez saw somebody on his turf who looked like an easy mark. He pulls Ames into the alley. Maybe there's a struggle. Maybe he's just in a bad mood. He's got the gun and he decides to lose the witness to the crime. This is one possible scenario.

SARA. And another? *(Pause.)*

WEBER. Miss McKeon, have you had any dinner?

SARA. No.

WEBER. I'm very hungry. Been on my feet since five-thirty this morning. Could I possibly interest you in — ?

SARA. I'm sorry. I would be horrible company.

WEBER. Sure.

SARA. The other scenario? *(Pause.)*

WEBER. It is very possible ... it is more than likely that your friend was involved in some ... illicit activities.

SARA. I see. *(Pause.)* Such as? *(Pause.)* What are we talking about? The mob? Narcotics? Child prostitution?

WEBER. I'm really not at liberty to say.

SARA. But you really *are* at liberty to insinuate.

WEBER. Now that is unfair.

SARA. To lose interest in the case, if that serves your purpose.

WEBER. If I have given you the impression —

SARA. What were all those questions about the other night?

WEBER. Miss McKeon —

SARA. And the girl? The suicide? Did you even check into that?

WEBER. We contacted all the hospitals in the area. There were no wrist-slashers brought in that week.

SARA. Then she was lying.

WEBER. Somebody was lying. *(Pause.)* Look. Miss McKeon. Go home. When I know more, I will call you on the telephone. I am sorry you don't appreciate our efforts. We will, however, find Emilio Sanchez. And when we do he will be tried and found guilty of the murder of David Ames.

SARA. How can you be so sure?

WEBER. Because I'm a cop. That is what I do for a living. What you do is write poems. I just want to make that distinction in case the lines were blurred for you. Now. I want you to remain uninvolved.

SARA. Do I appear to be uninvolved to you? *(Pause.)* Do I?

WEBER. Go home. *(He calls offstage.)* Al?

SARA. I don't understand. What were you going to say to me over dinner?

WEBER. What was I going to say? Probably I was going to say that I thought you were cute. Probably I was going to say that you have nice breasts. I'm sorry if this offends you, but that's the way I am. Probably I was going to offer to drive you home and then hopefully make a pass at you. But to tell you the truth, my heart isn't in it anymore. I'm sorry about your boyfriend. But, believe me, he's better off where he is. What you don't know about David Ames could fill volumes. I'm sorry you're taking this so badly. I would have thought someone of your obvious intelligence would have known better. Okay? Have I said enough? Can I go back to work now?

SARA. You're married.

WEBER. Me?

SARA. Yes.

WEBER. Yes. I'm married. I told you that. Oh, are you disappointed in me because I was considering cheating on my wife? Well. Life is full of contradictions. *(He shouts.)* DETECTIVE KERSNOWSKI!

SARA. How do you live with yourself?

WEBER. I don't have to. That's other people's prerogative. *(Kersnowski enters eating a donut.)* Al, would you be kind enough to drive Miss McKeon — ?

SARA. No. I can find my own way home. My God. My God, but you people disgust me. *(She moves to another part of the stage.)*

WEBER. I don't get it. What's not to like?

KERSNOWSKI. Beats me.

WEBER. You had dinner?

KERSNOWSKI. Yeah. *(Pause.)*

WEBER. You want to order *me* something?

Scene 7

Joyce enters as Weber and Kersnowski exit. She is carrying two coffee cups. She hands one to Sara. We are in the library again.

JOYCE. What do you think?

SARA. I think it's impossible. I think I would have known if there was something going on. Something hidden in his past. Or present.

JOYCE. This woman ...?

SARA. What?

JOYCE. This woman that he mentioned. You didn't know about her.

SARA. No. *(Pause.)* That's different. I can't tell you why.

JOYCE. I lived with this guy for three years. We were engaged. Going to be married in September. He teaches at the university where I went to school. Turns out he's been sleeping with most of the senior class. I never knew. I threw him out of the house. Literally. All of his belongings out on the street. A week ago this rock the size of my fist comes flying through the kitchen window. It's him. I know this. *(Pause.)* I thought it was love, Sara. Pure and unconditional.

SARA. It's not the same thing.

JOYCE. It never is. *(Sara puts down the cup and starts to walk away.)* Where are you going?

SARA. I don't know. *(Pause.)* I feel like I've become this freak suddenly. I mean, I lie down at night. Unable to sleep. Unable to ... stop thinking! Finally, I drift off. And I dream of him. Still breathing. Talking to me. Touching me. I wake up. And the cold, hard fact of his death hits me like a slap in the face. I become paralyzed by it. I force myself to get out of bed. To wash. To dress. To come here and pretend to be normal. Civilized. Unaffected.

JOYCE. Sara —

SARA. But I don't belong! Not here! And not there! I ... I ... oh, God. I can't explain it to you.

JOYCE. It's alright.

SARA. It's like part of me has gone away. *(Pause.)* He's gone. And part of me is lost. *(Pause.)* Jesus, I can't bear this god-awful self-pity. I mean, he's dead! Murdered! Shot in the back of the head like ... like an animal! Pushed into a garbage can! Left to rot!

JOYCE. It's not your fault.

SARA. Of course it's not my fault! WHY DO PEOPLE SAY SUCH STUPID THINGS? *(Silence.)* I'm sorry, Joyce. But there's nothing anybody can tell me that'll make me feel better. Except the truth. *(Pause.)* I have to know more. That's all. I ... simply have to know.

Scene 8

The sound of a subway train. Billy Hart enters as Joyce exits. He sets up bar. Sara stands at a distance observing him. Then she crosses and sits at the bar. We are in Billy Hart's Bar and Grill.

BILLY. What can I get you?

SARA. Um. A glass of wine, please. A burgundy.

BILLY. A burgundy. *(Billy looks behind the bar.)* Can't say I got anything like that back here. How about you let me mix you up something? Something with a little bite, but not too strong.

SARA. That would be fine. Thank you. *(He mixes her a drink.)*

BILLY. You'll pardon my saying so —

SARA. Yes?

BILLY. But you don't look like you belong around here. *(Pause.)*

SARA. No.

BILLY. Just passing through?

SARA. In a manner of speaking.

BILLY. Uh-huh. *(He serves her the drink.)* Now you try that. *(She does.)*

SARA. It's very good. *(Pause.)* What do you call it?

BILLY. I call it ... the potion. *(Pause. She takes another sip.)*

SARA. Have you been a bartender for a long time?

BILLY. Long as I been drinking. 'Fore that in point of fact, 'cause I used to tend the well at my Uncle John's place when I was just a kid, but I didn't take no crap, so I never got called out. Came here five years ago when the place was called The Pit. Honest. That was the name. Owner won't hire me at first 'cause he said I didn't have the personality of a bartender. Yeah, I thought, if only I had more personality maybe some of them derelicts over at John's wouldn't have puked up all over my shoes. But I worked a weekend and he hired me on. Next thing happens, I bust his fat ass in a card game, whereby he's forced to take me on as a partner. I borrow the money, buy him out, and change the name to Billy Hart's. That's a long answer to a short question, but it gives you some idea of the scope of my vision. *(Pause.)* Are you here for somebody?

SARA. No. *(Pause.)* I was a friend of David Ames.

BILLY. I don't know who that is.

SARA. He was murdered around the corner last week. The police think your cook may have committed the crime.

BILLY. Oh. *(Pause.)*

SARA. What do you think? Do you think that's possible?

BILLY. Sure. *(Pause.)*

SARA. Do you think that's what happened?

BILLY. Let me ask you something.

SARA. Alright.

BILLY. Is your name Angie?

SARA. No.

BILLY. You remind me of a girl I used to know named Angie.

SARA. How well did you know her?

BILLY. Not very well.

SARA. No?

BILLY. No. *(Pause.)* I saw her once across a crowded room. *(Pause.)* Does that answer your question? *(Pause.)* Sanchez worked here for seven months. I trusted him enough to lock the place up. I didn't trust him enough to walk my sister to night school. You hear what I'm saying? *(Pause.)* 'Nother drink?

SARA. Please. *(He pours.)* Did he lock up that night, Billy?

BILLY. Yeah.

SARA. So you left ...?

BILLY. Around one-thirty.

SARA. And the place was empty?

BILLY. Yeah ... no. *(Pause.)* No, I had three customers. Gal at the bar trying to get lucky. Two jokers playing pool.

SARA. Do you know these people?

BILLY. Nope. *(Pause.)*

SARA. So you left Sanchez ...?

BILLY. I gave him the keys. I walked out. That was the last I saw of the poor slob. *(Pause.)*

SARA. You liked him.

BILLY. Like? Like? Who likes anybody? Do you?

SARA. Some people.

BILLY. This ... fella? *(Pause.)*
SARA. Yeah. *(Pause.)*
BILLY. Emilio was okay. I wouldn't peg him to gut anybody. I don't know. I guess it happens. Got to find me a new cook. *(Sara finishes her drink.)*
SARA. Thank you.
BILLY. Drinks are on me.
SARA. Thanks. *(She gets up. She starts to go.)*
BILLY. So what's your name, anyway? *(She stops.)*
SARA. Sara. Sara McKeon.
BILLY. Sara? What is that? European?
SARA. Possibly.
BILLY. So what is it you do, Sara?
SARA. I'm a poet. *(Pause.)*
BILLY. Alright, so don't tell me.

Scene 9

Weber enters and sits at a table as Billy exits. Sara sits across from him. We are in a restaurant.

SARA. There were three people in the bar with Sanchez when Billy Hart left at one-thirty.
WEBER. Uh-huh.
SARA. Two men —
WEBER. Yes.
SARA. And a woman.
WEBER. I see.
SARA. And this fellow Sanchez —
WEBER. Right.
SARA. Who nobody can find.
WEBER. Not as of today.
SARA. Doesn't all this seem —
WEBER. Yes?
SARA. A little odd to you?
WEBER. Not exactly. No.
SARA. A little —

WEBER. Sara?

SARA. Too easy?

WEBER. Miss McKeon?

SARA. What?

WEBER. What are you doing?

SARA. I am attempting to reconstruct the events of that night.

WEBER. I see. And where did you learn how to do this? A comic book? The late show? *(Pause.)* You shouldn't have gone to Hart's.

SARA. Why not?

WEBER. Because it is a putrid neighborhood. Because it is the one place I can think of where dropping the bomb might actually be considered gentrification. *(Pause.)* Can we order now?

SARA. You're not being very helpful.

WEBER. What can I tell you? You know everything I know.

SARA. I don't think that's true.

WEBER. Miss McKeon. Sara. Why did you ask me to dinner?

SARA. Because I thought you were cute. Because I thought you had nice breasts. *(Pause.)* I want to know what it is you think David was involved in.

WEBER. There I cannot help you.

SARA. Why is that?

WEBER. Because it is another matter entirely.

SARA. Confidential?

WEBER. You could say that.

SARA. I don't believe you.

WEBER. Well, if you don't believe me now, wait till you see the can of worms.

SARA. I'd like to see that can of worms. *(Pause.)* I can pay you. I can give you money. *(He smiles.)*

WEBER. You couldn't afford me. *(Pause.)* Look, Miss McKeon, I don't want your money.

SARA. What is it you want? *(Pause.)* Do you want to go to bed with me?

WEBER. That is a very stupid thing to say.

SARA. I want to know.

WEBER. Why? Why is all this so important to you?

SARA. Because I think it's the reason that Emilio Sanchez has not been located. And the reason you're so indifferent to the fact that a man has been murdered. *(Pause.)*

WEBER. Are you familiar with the name Madison Lapointe?

SARA. Yes. He ... he's the real estate tycoon.

WEBER. Correct.

SARA. His wife and child were kidnapped last year. They were held for ransom.

WEBER. Two point five million dollars.

SARA. I remember.

WEBER. And the money was paid.

SARA. Right.

WEBER. And Emily Lapointe and her little girl were found dead ten days later. Beaten severely. Raped. And dead. *(Pause.)* I was put in charge of a task force to apprehend the killers. The physical evidence suggests that there were three of them. Three men. A month ago I got a lead which turned the case around. It led me to one person. *(Pause.)*

SARA. No. *(Pause.)* No, it's just not possible.

WEBER. It is more than possible.

SARA. He wouldn't do something like that. He ... he couldn't.

WEBER. Look, I realize, from your perspective —

SARA. You're talking about someone that you don't know. That you never even met!

WEBER. This is true, but —

SARA. David Ames was not a killer!

WEBER. A little louder, maybe. I think some people at the salad bar may have missed it.

SARA. It's the truth.

WEBER. And how do you know this to be a fact?

SARA. Because I know. Because I could not have ... done what I did. Felt what I still feel if it were true.

WEBER. You only knew him —

SARA. It doesn't matter.

WEBER. Two months, Sara.

SARA. It doesn't matter! Don't you understand? That's what I'm trying to — !

WEBER. Would you please calm down?

SARA. No! What you're talking about is fiction! Facts to accommodate your circumstances! But I know what is real! Here, God damn it! Here! *(She hits herself in the chest.)* Because if what you say is true — !

WEBER. Then you'd have been duped. Then this world would be a pretty rotten place to live in. Which it is. *(She stares at him. Then she gets up and leaves the table.)* Sara! Miss McKeon! *(Sara exits. A moment. Weber shakes his head.)* Nice going, slick.

Scene 10

Weber exits. The sound of traffic. Sara enters, crosses to a bench and sits. A moment. Then Kersnowski enters. He approaches her. We are at a bus stop.

SARA. What?

KERSNOWSKI. He wants me to see that you get home safely.

SARA. I'm fine.

KERSNOWSKI. That's what I told him.

SARA. I'm waiting for the bus.

KERSNOWSKI. I said that, too. He said I should give you a lift.

SARA. No. Thank you.

KERSNOWSKI. I'll just wait with you. *(He sits. Silence.)* I don't get up into this part of town much. Seems alright. Book stores. Movie houses. What's that over there?

SARA. Where?

KERSNOWSKI. There. *(He points.)*

SARA. That's a club.

KERSNOWSKI. A club?

SARA. For dancing.

KERSNOWSKI. They dance in there? *(He stares.)* Boy, you can't tell that from the outside. Somebody's not using their head. *(Pause.)* I'm real sorry about what happened to your friend, Miss McKeon. I lost my kid brother 'bout this time last year. He was a cop. He was pulling over some junkie for run-

28

ning a red light. Guy gets out of the car and nails him with an automatic. They kept him on a respirator for three weeks. Then they let him go. *(Pause. Kersnowski reaches into his coat pocket and removes something in a wrapper. He looks at it.)* I got half a candy bar here. You want that? *(Sara shakes her head.)* Thought you might be hungry. H.E. says you didn't eat no dinner.

SARA. H. E.?

KERSNOWSKI. Weber. *(Pause.)* You don't like him much, huh?

SARA. No.

KERSNOWSKI. He likes you. I can tell. *(Pause.)* I know he's kind of hard around the edges. And he's got a bad disposition and a mean temper. And he cheats on the wife and does deals and sometimes he beats people up. But besides that, he's a pretty good guy.

SARA. What is the law, Detective? What is this ... this line that we have drawn? Does it mean anything? Does it represent us in any way? What is it?

KERSNOWSKI. The law? *(He shrugs.)* I guess it's what keeps us from tearing each other up more than we already do. *(Pause.)* Here's your bus.

Scene 11

David enters as Kersnowski exits. David sits down and begins to look over his books. Sara rises and moves toward him. She puts her arms around him from behind. He leans back into her. They kiss. We are in Sara's apartment.

SARA. What are you doing?

DAVID. Going over my receipts.

SARA. And?

DAVID. And I need more money.

SARA. Whatever for?

DAVID. Well, from what I understand, it's the going means of exchange.

SARA. But you're doing well.

DAVID. I need to be doing better. Much, much, much better.

SARA. And what would you do with these additional resources, hmm?

DAVID. Well, I'd start by digging myself out of debt. I've got a couple of regular customers I would dearly love to lose. I'd double the waitstaff. Do some advertising. Hire a chef who knows how to prepare something besides a three-minute egg.

SARA. Boring.

DAVID. Alright, then. I'd take you away.

SARA. Better.

DAVID. I'd buy you nice things.

SARA. I don't want nice things.

DAVID. I'd buy them anyway. Diamond earrings. Long, satin gowns.

SARA. I'd look ridiculous.

DAVID. I'd publish your poems.

SARA. Ah, well. There's something.

DAVID. You could quit the library.

SARA. I don't mind it there.

DAVID. Oh, Sara.

SARA. I don't.

DAVID. There's something wrong with you.

SARA. I don't think so.

DAVID. No. You're abnormal. It is abnormal *not* to be immersed in the greed of this society.

SARA. Well. You're not.

DAVID. No. I am. I'm in it up to my — *(She hands him a book.)* What's this?

SARA. A gift.

DAVID. Oh, Sara. You shouldn't buy me presents.

SARA. Why not?

DAVID. Because you have no money.

SARA. I have plenty of money.

DAVID. You have nothing.

SARA. "Desire for nothing ... "

DAVID. "Except desirelessness." Yes, well, for us mere human people that can be a little difficult. *(He looks at the book.)* Dylan Thomas? Wasn't he a drunk?

SARA. And a fornicator. Read where I've marked. *(He does.)*

DAVID. "They are the only dead who did not love,
Lipless and tongueless in the sour earth
Staring at others, poor unlovers.
They are the only living thing who did love,
So are we full with strength,
Ready to rise, easy to sleep." *(Pause.)* That's a nice poem. Nice ... sentiment. Really. *(Pause.)* Not as good as yours, of course. *(She laughs.)* But I like it.

SARA. Can I say something?

DAVID. Anything.

SARA. I think you should consider leaving the restaurant.

DAVID. What do you mean?

SARA. Leave it. Walk out. The work makes you unhappy.

DAVID. Well, that's what work is designed to do. That's its function. If it wasn't causing tremendous physical and mental fatigue, then it wouldn't be serving its purpose.

SARA. Leave the restaurant and we'll sail around the world.

DAVID. On what? Our good looks?

SARA. We could find a way.

DAVID. You honestly believe that, don't you?

SARA. I do.

DAVID. You're a crazy woman.

SARA. We could do it, David. We could brave the elements. See it all.

DAVID. Tell you what. *(Pause.)* Some money's coming through. It's a slow process. I don't want to bore you with the details. But if it happens ... when it happens, we could take some time off.

SARA. I don't mean a vacation. I mean ... go somewhere else. Get away from this economic cancer that cripples the best in us.

DAVID. What ... to live?

SARA. To live. To breathe freely. To run naked in the sand.

DAVID. Well, now you've roused my interest. *(She laughs.)*

SARA. So what do you think?

DAVID. I think it's an attractive proposition.

SARA. But what?

DAVID. But nothing. It's an attractive proposition. I'd like to sleep on it. With you. *(She laughs.)* You know what I like about you, Sara? The thing I admire the most?

SARA. No. Tell me.

DAVID. You never think small. See, other people, women, whatever, they get their heads stuck in the garbage and the decay. They get caught down there. Trapped. They can't move. They shrivel up. Shrink. Dreams and all. They just ... die away. But you. I mean, your head's always in the clouds. Not in a bad way, either, but like that's where you're meant to be. Thinking up. Elevated. Thinking ... big. *(Pause.)* I didn't say that very well.

SARA. No. No, you said it beautifully. Thank you. *(David looks back at the book in his hands.)*

DAVID. "Only dead ... who did not love." See, this guy knew how to talk.

SARA. Just one thing.

DAVID. What's that?

SARA. He's dead. *(David smiles. They kiss. He pulls her into his body.)*

Scene 12

A telephone rings. David exits. He leaves the book in Sara's hands. She stares at it. Weber enters. Sara moves to answer the phone. Weber is on the other line. He holds a bottle of beer in his hand. We are in Sara's apartment.

SARA. Hello?

WEBER. It's Weber. *(Pause.)* Sorry to ruin an otherwise perfect evening. You got home alright?

SARA. Yes.

WEBER. That's good. I just ... I wanted to make sure. *(Pause.)*

SARA. Where are you?

WEBER. At a bar. My kids are having a slumber party. They

asked me to leave the house. *(Pause.)* Look, Sara, I'm sorry about what I said earlier. I had no right to tell you that stuff.
SARA. I pushed you into it.
WEBER. Regardless. It was bad form on my part. I apologize. *(Pause.)*
SARA. What does the "H" stand for?
WEBER. What?
SARA. H. E. Weber? *(Pause.)*
WEBER. Horace.
SARA. Horace?
WEBER. We don't need to make a big thing about this, okay?
SARA. Okay.
WEBER. Alright. You call me if you need anything.
SARA. I will. Goodnight. *(She hangs up. Weber exits as Eisenstadt enters. A moment. The phone rings again. She answers it. Eisenstadt is on the other line.)* Weber?
EISENSTADT. No. That is not my name. *(Pause.)*
SARA. Who is this?
EISENSTADT. Is this the McKeon residence? Sara McKeon?
SARA. Yes.
EISENSTADT. I understand you are looking for some information. I would very much like to talk to you. *(Pause.)* Would you like to talk to me? *(Pause.)*
SARA. Yes.
EISENSTADT. Good. Where will you be at four o'clock tomorrow afternoon?
SARA. At the Cultural Center. I'm doing a reading.
EISENSTADT. Oh. Some of your poetry? *(Pause.)*
SARA. No. The work of another writer.
EISENSTADT. And who, may I ask, will be represented?
SARA. I am reading the poems of Dylan Thomas.
EISENSTADT. I am not familiar with his work. I shall attend the concert. And afterwards we will go to the park. I do look forward to it, Miss McKeon.
SARA. How did you — ?
EISENSTADT. Goodnight. *(Eisenstadt hangs up. Sara holds the telephone in her hand.)*

Scene 13

Eisenstadt exits. Sara crosses to the center of the stage. She reads from the book. She addresses the audience.

SARA. "This side of the truth
You may not see, my son,
King of your blue eyes
In the blinding country of youth,
That all is undone,
Under the unminding skies,
Of innocence and guilt
Before you move to make
One gesture of the heart or head,
Is gathered and spilt
Into the winding dark
Like the dust of the dead.

Good and bad, two ways
Of moving about your death
By the grinding sea,
King of your heart in the blind days,
Blow away like breath,
Go crying through you and me
And the souls of all men
Into the innocent
Dark, and the guilty dark, and good
Death, and bad death, and then
In the last element,
Fly like the stars' blood,

Like the sun's tears,
Like the moon's seed, rubbish
And fire, the flying rant
Of the sky, king of your six years.
And the wicked wish,
Down the beginning of plants

34

And animals and birds,
Water and light, the earth and sky,
Is cast before you move,
And all your deeds and words,
Each truth, each lie,
Die in unjudging love."
(The sound of two hands clapping. Eisenstadt enters and crosses to Sara. She closes the book. She turns and looks at him. He extends his hand.)
EISENSTADT.   My name is Carl Eisenstadt.

Scene 14

The sound of birds chirping. Children laughing. Sara and Eisenstadt sit together on a bench. She carries the book with her. We are in the park.

EISENSTADT.   Well. Your performance was very good.
SARA.   Thank you.
EISENSTADT.   Very well received. By those who were there. Tell me, why do so few people attend?
SARA.   I'm not sure, exactly. I suppose it's something of an elitist art form.
EISENSTADT.   Ah, yes. The strange case of modern poetry. Do you know, I read somewhere that there are more people writing poems these days than reading them. What does that signify, do you imagine? The death of language?
SARA.   Perhaps.
EISENSTADT.   I think so. People no longer see it as an effective tool. To get what they want. Yes, of course, it serves to express an idea. But ideas are really not important. You cannot pay the rent with an idea. We are more concerned with getting what we want. No?
SARA.   Yes. *(Pause.)* What is it you want?
EISENSTADT.   I was acquainted with your friend.
SARA.   David?
EISENSTADT.   Yes.

SARA. Under what circumstances?

EISENSTADT. That I do not care to discuss.

SARA. Were you part of the kidnapping? *(Eisenstadt looks at her. Silence.)*

EISENSTADT. What kidnapping, Miss McKeon?

SARA. The kidnapping of Emily Lapointe and her daughter. And their subsequent murder.

EISENSTADT. Oh, yes. I read about that in the newspaper. Terrible incident. Now, why would you think that I was a part of that atrocity?

SARA. I was told that there were three men involved. That David may actually have been one of them.

EISENSTADT. Who? Who told you this?

SARA. The police.

EISENSTADT. Oh, the police. Goodness me. For a minute I thought you had some serious source. Well, Miss McKeon, I cannot speak for your friend, but I myself was out of the country during the time that this occurred.

SARA. You were?

EISENSTADT. Yes, indeed.

SARA. And you read about it in the newspaper? Out of the country? *(Pause.)*

EISENSTADT. You are too literal, Miss McKeon. It is the fault of an over-educated mind. I heard about these crimes.

SARA. And the death of David Ames?

EISENSTADT. He was robbed, was he not?

SARA. That is one theory.

EISENSTADT. It will suffice.

SARA. You seem quite satisfied by it. Almost glad.

EISENSTADT. Glad? *(He shrugs.)* I have no grief, if that is what you mean. It would be wrong to say that I did.

SARA. What information were you going to give me, Mr. Eisenstadt? What is the point of this meeting?

EISENSTADT. Only this. Your friend is dead. And you are still young. You must go on. Find another. Do not let this sad circumstance obsess you.

SARA. Where is Emilio Sanchez? *(Pause.)*

EISENSTADT. When your Mr. Thomas says: "The force that

through the green fuse drives the flower drives my green age,"
now, what does he mean by that?
SARA. You are changing the subject.
EISENSTADT. I had hoped you would notice.
SARA. I am going to find out what happened to David Ames.
EISENSTADT. But it has already been explained.
SARA. Not to my satisfaction.
EISENSTADT. Language. It really is a problem.
SARA. Who else was involved in the Lapointe kidnapping?
EISENSTADT. He died rather young, didn't he? Your Mr.
Thomas? Such a shame. And the American woman. This Sylvia
Plath. I understand that she was only thirty years of age. What
do you suppose happens to them? These poets? Is it possible
that they are something of an anachronism? That they discover
this and can no longer live with themselves? Or is it, perhaps,
a deathwish? Do they place themselves within a profession that
leads to tragic results? It is an interesting question, I think.
The idea of the deathwish. *(Pause.)* Please, would you auto-
graph my program?

Scene 15

*David enters, dressing hurriedly, as Eisenstadt exits. We are
in Sara's apartment.*

SARA. Where are you going?
DAVID. Work. City health inspector's coming by today. Some-
body's got to be there to pay him off.
SARA. Don't go.
DAVID. I have to.
SARA. Don't.
DAVID. Sara — *(He turns and looks at her. A moment.)* Don't
look at me that way.
SARA. What way?
DAVID. You know very well what way. That ... that little, lost,
innocent, temptress expression you get on your face.
SARA. Me?

37

DAVID. Yes. You. You know exactly what it is you're doing.

SARA. What am I doing? *(She moves toward him. She kisses him.)*

DAVID. Sara, if we start, I'll never get out of here.

SARA. Let's start.

DAVID. Sara — *(She kisses him again.)* This isn't fair.

SARA. I don't mean to be fair. I mean to be unfair. Wicked, in fact.

DAVID. Listen, I am entering a state of arousal here that's going to be difficult to talk myself out of.

SARA. Take me to that state.

DAVID. I will. I will. But later.

SARA. Now.

DAVID. Sara. Sara McKeon. I really, really do have to go. *(A moment. She smiles and moves away from him.)*

SARA. Alright. One condition.

DAVID. You got it.

SARA. Come home early.

DAVID. I will. I'll do my best.

SARA. And let yourself in. *(She tosses him a set of keys. He catches them. He looks at them.)*

DAVID. Keys.

SARA. To the apartment.

DAVID. Uh-huh. *(Pause.)* Well. Thanks. *(She laughs.)*

SARA. They're not a contract, David. I just thought they might make things easier.

DAVID. Right. *(Pause.)*

SARA. What is it?

DAVID. You're too trusting, Miss McKeon. You trust people entirely too much.

SARA. I trust you. Is that bad?

DAVID. No. *(Pause.)* Sara, how long have we ... known each other? *(She shrugs.)* Less than two weeks.

SARA. So? This is true love, isn't it?

DAVID. Yes. Yes, it is.

SARA. Are you going to rob me blind?

DAVID. No.

SARA. Break my heart?

DAVID. Absolutely not.

SARA. So what are you afraid of?

DAVID. What am I afraid of? *(Pause.)* I'm afraid of myself, I guess. Of my capacity to cause ... pain. *(Pause.)* Look, I don't want anything to happen. I don't want anything to go wrong. But it could.

SARA. What do you mean?

DAVID. Something could go wrong.

SARA. Is that what you're intending?

DAVID. No. I've told you. It's the last thing on my mind.

SARA. Oh, God, David, don't make me feel stupid about this.

DAVID. I'm sorry. I don't mean to.

SARA. Give me the keys.

DAVID. No.

SARA. Give me the keys if it makes you —

DAVID. Sara. Please. Just ... just listen to me. *(Pause.)* I don't know why, but ... I've had what you might refer to as rotten luck in the past.

SARA. With women? *(He laughs.)*

DAVID. With life. In general. In specific, I could point to a lousy upbringing in a rat-infested neighborhood, a bad attitude that got me into trouble more often than I would care to admit, and a series of dead-end career opportunities that took me nowhere real fast. But what the hell. You make your own luck. So. So here I am holding something in my hands that could actually make a difference. That really means something to me. I don't want to blow it.

SARA. So. Don't. *(Pause.)*

DAVID. Right.

SARA. This is a first for me, too, you know.

DAVID. What is?

SARA. You. Here. The keys. All of it. I ... *(Pause.)* I don't know what to say. *(Pause.)* David, I'm going to ask you something. And you have to tell me the truth. Even if you think I don't want to hear it. *(Pause.)*

DAVID. Okay.

SARA. Do you think we should stop?

DAVID. No. *(Pause.)* No, I don't think we should stop.

SARA. 'Cause I'm real frightened, here.

DAVID. Me, too.

SARA. Yeah?

DAVID. Yeah. *(Pause.)*

SARA. Would you hold me? *(He goes to her. He holds her. A moment.)*

DAVID. Sara?

SARA. What? *(He laughs.)*

DAVID. Nothing. *(Pause.)* I'm just ... overwhelmed, you know? You overwhelm me.

SARA. That's nice.

DAVID. No. Honestly. I'm in awe.

SARA. Of me?

DAVID. Of your willingness to throw yourself into the life of a stranger. *(She looks at him.)*

SARA. You're no stranger to me. *(He laughs.)* You're not.

DAVID. Okay. But there are things about me ... many things that you don't know.

SARA. Things. I know you. *(Pause.)* I know you.

Scene 16

The sound of a police siren. Weber comes running on as David moves to another part of the stage. David's eyes stay on Sara. We are still in her apartment.

WEBER. What happened?

SARA. I —

WEBER. Tell me what happened.

SARA. I'm not sure.

WEBER. Tell me what you think.

SARA. There was someone. In the dark. When I came home. In the kitchen. I heard him breathing. *(Kersnowski rushes in with his gun drawn.)*

KERSNOWSKI. Back door's open.

WEBER. Did you see who it was?

SARA. No.

KERSNOWSKI. You should have got out.

40

SARA. I couldn't ... move.

WEBER. You did right to call me.

KERSNOWSKI. I'll check the alley. *(Kersnowski exits. David exits another way.)*

WEBER. Are you alright? *(She nods.)* Christ, Sara.

SARA. I just ... froze.

WEBER. You did okay.

SARA. He could have killed me.

WEBER. We don't know that. It might have been a burglary.

SARA. Eisenstadt.

WEBER. Who?

SARA. I met a man named Eisenstadt today. He made some threats. *(Pause.)* Do you know this person? *(Pause.)*

WEBER. Oh, yeah. I got a file two inches thick on his activities. Why did he come to you?

SARA. He telephoned me. We met in the park.

WEBER. Jesus God.

SARA. I think he was involved in the Lapointe kidnapping.

WEBER. Uh-huh. And you know this ... how?

SARA. Because he had an alibi which was paper thin. And because of his behavior. And the look in his eyes. It was transparent. *(Pause.)* I think you should bring him in for questioning.

WEBER. Sara. Let me tell you something about Carl "The Iceman" Eisenstadt. Do you know what he does for a living? He cuts people's throats. He is very, very good at it. He is so good, as a matter of fact, that in fifteen years of performing this function he has never once been caught without a good excuse. He is a fish. He is the king of the slice and dice club. In short, he is a very bad man. And you had lunch with him?

SARA. He said he knew David.

WEBER. This I do not doubt. This has the ring of authenticity. Christ, Almighty.

SARA. I think you should arrest him.

WEBER. Listen to me, Sara McKeon. This is no longer an academic matter. I want you to hang it up. Do you hear me? These are bad people who are coming to you. And I will not have it.

SARA. David Ames was innocent.

WEBER. David Ames was a first-class, A number one crook! He was garbage! He was walking crud!

SARA. You have no proof.

WEBER. Sara, what did he do for a living? He owned a restaurant. A very nice establishment on top of one of the hottest pieces of real estate in town. How did he get the money to buy that location? Hmm?

SARA. He ... he told me he borrowed it.

WEBER. AND WHO DID HE BORROW IT FROM? *(Pause.)* That's right, Sara. The big boys. Now. I don't know if you've noticed, but business at the Fast Track ain't been too good. So what does he do? He goes in on a heroin deal. Which proceeds to fall apart. Now he's in double jeopardy. He's got two guns pointed at both knees. So he comes up with a plan to cut all his losses. I'm not saying he masterminded the operation. But he certainly owned one third of the doorprize.

SARA. It makes no sense.

WEBER. It makes a lot of sense. He was a desperate man in a bad situation. He may not have meant for the killings to happen. But that's how it fell out.

SARA. This is all speculation.

WEBER. My department put markers on the bills that Lapointe paid to the kidnappers. Special serial numbers. A month ago we get a call says a lot of these bills are coming out of the Fast Track. *(Pause.)* He was laundering money through the restaurant, Sara. *(Pause.)* We went into his apartment after the murder. Found a suitcase full of cash in the back of the closet. All with numbers on our sheets. *(Pause.)* The kidnapping took place over three days in December. Guess where David Ames was that weekend? At home with the flu. Nobody talked to him. Nobody saw him. *(Pause.)* Do you want me to go on?

SARA. No. *(Pause.)*

WEBER. Is there somebody you can stay with? Somebody they wouldn't know about? 'Cause I think this place is a bad idea right now.

SARA. There's a girl at work.

WEBER. Why don't you pack some things? I'll take you there. *(Sara doesn't move.)* Sara? *(Pause.)* Sara, I'm sorry I had to tell you all this. *(She looks up at him.)*
SARA. No, you're not. *(They stand in place. Looking at each other. A moment.)*
WEBER. You're right. I'm not.

Scene 17

The sound of a subway train. Billy Hart enters as Weber exits. He sets up shop. Sara stands at a distance. Billy looks up. We are in Billy Hart's Bar and Grill.

SARA. Still serving?
BILLY. For you? Anytime. *(She crosses to the bar and sits down.)* What can I get you?
SARA. Something strong. Something that'll make me stop thinking.
BILLY. That's a tall order.
SARA. Should I take my business elsewhere?
BILLY. Nope. *(He pours her a shot of whiskey. She takes it back.)*
SARA. Again, please. *(He pours. She drinks.)* Again.
BILLY. That's some kind of thirst you've got there.
SARA. There's a lot of noise in my head. I intend to drown it out.
BILLY. Uh-huh. *(He pours.)* This wouldn't have anything to do with your boyfriend, would it? *(A moment.)* Sorry I asked. *(She drinks. A moment.)*
SARA. It would appear that David Ames ... the man I loved ... was a killer. That he led a double life of which I had no knowledge. That he lied to me from the start. And that none of these things showed up in the way he looked at me. In the way he talked to me. In the way he touched me. *(Pause.)*
BILLY. Not exactly a pretty story.
SARA. Yes, well, the pretty stories are filling slim volumes these days. Again. *(He pours. She drinks.)* I haven't lost faith. I really haven't. It's just that the world begins to run you down,

you know?

BILLY. I know.

SARA. There was a time I thought that education was everything.

BILLY. It is.

SARA. No. It'll only get you so far. Everyone complains about the school system in this country, but you know what?

BILLY. What's that?

SARA. They could have a better system if they wanted. Hell, they put a man on the moon, didn't they?

BILLY. So I hear.

SARA. But they don't want it. Because knowledge is devalued currency.

BILLY. It is.

SARA. People want money. They don't want morality. Or art. Or justice. They just want money.

BILLY. There you go. *(Pause.)*

SARA. Is that what a bartender does?

BILLY. What's that?

SARA. Agrees with everything that's said?

BILLY. Absolutely. *(She laughs.)* That's nice.

SARA. What is?

BILLY. Hearing you laugh. *(Pause.)* 'Nother drink?

SARA. Yes. I'd like eighteen whiskies, please.

BILLY. That's a lot of liquor.

SARA. Stacked up into a pyramid.

BILLY. Any particular reason?

SARA. That's what Dylan Thomas ordered the night he drank himself to death.

BILLY. Oh. *(He pours.)* Thomas, huh?

SARA. Played for the Bears.

BILLY. Yeah, I remember now. *(She lifts her glass.)*

SARA. A toast. *(He lifts the bottle.)* "Though lovers be lost love shall not."

BILLY. "And death shall have no dominion." *(He clinks the bottle against her glass.)* And here you thought I was just an ignorant slob. *(Silence.)*

SARA. I miss him so much. *(A moment.)* I wish I'd been here that night.

BILLY. Let it go, Sara.

SARA. I do wish it.

BILLY. Believe me. It was nothing special.

SARA. Two jokers playing pool.

BILLY. That's right.

SARA. Some gal at the bar trying to get lucky.

BILLY. Did I say that? *(She nods.)* Well, she was, too. Kept staring at the door all night. Waiting for something to walk in. Chain smoking cigarettes like there was no tomorrow. She just held 'em in her hand till they burnt down to her glove. I said, "Lady, you might want to put that ash out 'fore you catch your hand on fire." *(Pause.)*

SARA. Gloves?

BILLY. Yeah. Almost like mittens. Crazy broad.

SARA. In August?

BILLY. What?

SARA. Who wears gloves in August?

BILLY. I don't know.

SARA. Unless you're covering something up. Your hands. *(Pause.)* Your wrists. *(Pause.)* Oh, my God. Oh, Jesus.

Scene 18

Marie enters as Billy exits. Sara turns to her. We are in a hotel room. Marie has bandages around both of her wrists.

MARIE. How did you find me?

SARA. I spoke to David's father. He let me look through an old address book. Go through some photographs. I went to the Fast Track and got a list of the people who've worked there. I asked a lot of questions. The name Marie kept coming back. Marie Defaria. They said you worked at the restaurant. As a cashier. You left in the spring. Since then you've had no fixed address. But the janitor in your mother's building thought he heard you might be living in some hotel. This is the closest thing I could find to match that description in the neighborhood of Billy Hart's.

MARIE. Me and David. We had a falling out.

SARA. That's what I understand. What happened?

MARIE. He didn't want me no more. *(Pause.)*

SARA. The night he was killed —

MARIE. Yeah?

SARA. You telephoned him. *(Pause.)* Do you want to tell me why?

MARIE. No.

SARA. If you tell me then someone else will know. *(Pause.)*

MARIE. They came to my place. My girlfriend's apartment.

SARA. Who?

MARIE. Two men.

SARA. For what?

MARIE. They said they were friends of David's. Said he owed them some money. *(Pause.)*

SARA. What did they want you to do, Marie?

MARIE. To call him. To say there was an emergency and I needed to see him. That I'd tried to kill myself. I said he wouldn't believe me. That I would never do such a thing. *(Pause.)* They take me into the bathroom. The one with the jewelry, he holds my arms out over the bathtub. The old guy takes out a knife. He pulls it across one of my wrists. Then the other one. Then blood started coming out and I was screaming. I passed out. When I woke up there were bandages on both my arms and the one fella is putting something back in his bag. Like medical equipment. The one with the knife is smoking a cigarette. He says, "Well, Marie. He'll believe you now." *(Pause.)* I call David. I tell him to meet me at the bar and grill. I put on these gloves and, the three of us, we go there. They tell me to take a seat. Then they go in the back to shoot a game a pool like nothing's going on, but they're watching me the whole time. David walks in. He sees me. He doesn't see them. He sits down and we're talking. I feel sick in the pit of my stomach, but I don't know what to do. Then the guy with the jewelry starts walking toward us. David sees me looking and he turns around. The guy pulls out a gun. I yell something and the Mexican comes out of the back. The

46

old guy has his knife out and goes for him. I start running towards the door. I hear the gun go off. I keep running. I don't turn around. Then there's two shots behind me. Like someone in the street. I keep running. *(Pause.)* I read about it the next day. The way they found his body. I tried to think what I did wrong. Besides wanting to stay alive. *(Pause.)*

SARA. These men?

MARIE. Yeah?

SARA. Do you remember their names? *(Pause.)* The one with the knife?

MARIE. Carl.

SARA. Carl Eisenstadt?

MARIE. That's it. And the other one sounded like a girl. Julie.

SARA. Julie? Julian? *(Pause.)* Julius?

MARIE. Julius Gatz. That's his name.

Scene 19

Gatz enters as Marie exits. He sits at a table with an empty chair facing him. We are in another restaurant. Sara sits down in the empty chair. Gatz looks at her.

GATZ. Why are you sitting at my table?

SARA. I know who you are.

GATZ. That's very nice. I don't believe I've had the pleasure.

SARA. I'm a friend of David Ames.

GATZ. Really? I'm a friend of Barney Giancarlos.

SARA. I don't know who that is.

GATZ. Now we're even. *(Pause.)* I'm supposed to know this guy? *(Pause.)* Would it be alright if I eat while we talk?

SARA. Your name is Julius Gatz.

GATZ. And your name is ...?

SARA. I'm onto you. I know what you do for a living, Mr. Gatz.

GATZ. Is that right? Would you pass me the mustard sauce?

SARA. I've spoken with Eisenstadt.

GATZ. Is that a fact?

SARA. Yes, it is.

GATZ. Who's Eisenstadt?

SARA. Eisenstadt and Gatz. Gatz and Eisenstadt. The names seem connected in this part of town like Leopold and Loeb.

GATZ. See, now, them I've heard of.

SARA. It's how I found you. "Always eats at the same restaurant. Seven o'clock. Every night."

GATZ. Sometimes six-thirty. I like to shake people up a little.

SARA. Tell me, Mr. Gatz, were you having dinner at this table two weeks ago Monday night?

GATZ. Monday? Let's see. Yes. I do believe so.

SARA. I don't. I think you were at the home of Marie Defaria. I think you held down her arms while Eisenstadt sliced open her wrists. I think you forced her into telephoning David Ames. Who you then murdered. Also Emilio Sanchez.

GATZ. Let me check that for you. *(He pulls a little black book out of his coat pocket and thumbs through it.)* What did you say this broad's name was? Oh, yeah. Here we go. "Wrist-slashing at Marie's." Boy, that was some night. And here I'd forgotten all about it. *(He replaces the book.)* Is there anything else you'd like to talk about before you go?

SARA. Emily Lapointe and her little girl. *(Pause.)*

GATZ. This conversation is beginning to put me off my goulash. *(Pause.)* Is there something specific I can do for you?

SARA. You can sweat a little. You can give something away in the sound of your voice. As you did just now.

GATZ. Yeah, well, lady, I don't know who you're sleeping with to get your bits and pieces, but these kind of ugly accusations don't carry much firepower in my neighborhood.

SARA. No?

GATZ. No.

SARA. We'll find out. You think you live outside the law. You don't.

GATZ. Well, this has been a real swell date. Thanks so much for stopping by.

SARA. I'm going to get you, Gatz. I don't know how, but I'm going to see you buried.

GATZ. What a lovely sentiment. Thank you. *(She gets up to leave.)* Oh, Miss McKeon? Sara? *(She turns.)* Do you get any vacation time at the library? *(Pause.)* 'Cause I would recommend you use it. Take two weeks. Longer, perhaps. Frankly, Sara, you seem kind of ... frazzled. Like you don't know what you might bump into. So take my advice. Go on holiday, okay? I say this as a way of saving you from yourself. *(Pause.)*
SARA. I have no intention —
GATZ. It's time to go now.

Scene 20

Joyce enters as Gatz exits. Sara turns to her. We are in Joyce's apartment.

JOYCE. You're insane.
SARA. I am gathering the pieces.
JOYCE. You did what?
SARA. Weber will listen to me. When I have the right evidence.
JOYCE. You're not going out there again.
SARA. I am. I *have* to see Billy Hart.
JOYCE. Sara, the whole point in your being here with me was to hide you from these psychopaths. It completely defeats the purpose if you continue to make dinner engagements with them. *(Sara explodes.)*
SARA. I am sick of being hidden! I am fed up with behaving well! I am so tired of fear and ignorance and the feeling in my gut of utter uselessness! I hate this state! This dream state I've created! I close up! I hear nothing! I see some kind of a perfect world which exists nowhere I can find! AND I'M DONE WITH IT! *(Pause.)* A man died. I thought I knew him. I continue to love him. And I will see this through. To my own end. To the end of my belief.
JOYCE. And what that killer said in the park? About a death-wish? Does that hold any meaning for you? *(Pause.)* I'm going with you.
SARA. No! *(Pause.)* No, now I am alone.

49

Scene 21

Billy enters as Joyce exits. Sara turns to him. We are in Billy Hart's Bar and Grill.

BILLY. You want me to do what?

SARA. Identify them. Testify. Tell enough to put them away forever.

BILLY. I don't know that much.

SARA. You were there. You saw them in the bar before you left that night.

BILLY. Yeah, but —

SARA. Just tell the truth.

BILLY. What about the girl? Why can't she tell the truth?

SARA. She's absolutely terrified, Billy. She won't talk. She won't even leave the hotel room. After they're picked up, she'll come forward. But not before. *(Pause.)* Is it too much to ask?

BILLY. Sara, these are major leaguers we're talking about here. Guys in my profession get turned into road-fill for a little loose lip. Who's to say they won't get off? Or get out in six months and come looking for me?

SARA. There are no guarantees, Billy.

BILLY. And what about my wife? My family?

SARA. I didn't know you were married.

BILLY. Not now, but someday I'd like to be. *(Pause.)* He means that much, huh?

SARA. Yes. *(Pause.)* He was kind to me. He listened when I spoke. He saw me and not the illusion I create. He understood my scribblings and read them again and again. He held me in the dark when I needed reassurance. He was the childhood I never had. The good death I dream of. He was my own life. My heart. My breath. My skin and bones. All of my sins and aspirations. Heaven and earth. Earth and sky. *(Pause.)* Will you?

Scene 22

Marie enters as Billy exits. Sara crosses to a telephone and picks it up. Marie picks up the other phone. We are again on opposite sides of a conversation.

SARA. Marie? *(Pause.)*

MARIE. Who is this?

SARA. It's Sara. Sara McKeon. *(Pause.)*

MARIE. What do you want?

SARA. Billy Hart is going to testify. I've talked to him. He'll come forward. He'll identify Gatz and Eisenstadt as the two men in the bar that night. I ... I wanted to call you. To say how very grateful I am for the information you gave me. Without you, I would have given up. I'm sure of it. But Hart will talk. These men'll be picked up. And then you'll be free to come out of hiding.

MARIE. Hart?

SARA. Yes. Billy Hart. The owner of the bar and grill. *(Pause.)* What's the matter, Marie? *(Pause.)* What's happened?

MARIE. Ain't you got a TV in your pretty, little, upscale apartment?

SARA. I —

MARIE. Don't you read the news?

SARA. What is it?

MARIE. Billy Hart is dead, Sara. Thanks for all your sympathy and good intentions. But Billy Hart is dead.

Scene 23

The sound of a subway train. Marie hangs up. Then Sara hangs up. Weber and Kersnowski enter as Marie exits. Sara turns to them. Weber is smoking a cigarette. We are in the backroom of the police station.

KERSNOWSKI. The train was an express. It was going right through the station at top speed. The driver says there was no

51

way he could have seen it coming. It was rush hour. The crowd was standing too close to the edge of the platform. He says he felt him under the train before he heard anything. And he never saw him fall.

SARA. Fall?

WEBER. He was pushed, Sara. Given a leave of absence. Poor, stupid son of a bitch. God damn it. GOD DAMN! *(Weber kicks something. He moves across the room. He looks out a window.)* Have I mentioned to either of you how much I hate this neighborhood?

KERSNOWSKI. I think so. Yes.

WEBER. The stench of it? The way it sticks under your feet? The rotting architecture? The grey faces? The way when the sun comes out you can't even tell the difference?

KERSNOWSKI. What do you want to do?

WEBER. What I want to do is start life over. What I *will* do is crack this thing wide open. Big enough to see the guts and insides. Sara, we've got to talk to the girl. You need to tell us where she is.

SARA. I know. *(Pause. Weber goes to her.)*

WEBER. Don't take it so hard.

SARA. It's my fault. I went too far.

WEBER. Listen to me. Not everything that happens to people is your responsibility. Not everything is explainable. You keep trying to make sense of it, don't you?

SARA. Yes.

WEBER. Stop that. I learned a long time ago there ain't no such thing as an even deal. Justice, when it happens, is an accident. Got it?

SARA. Yes.

WEBER. That way you can sleep at night on small rewards. Now. I'm going to take you to your girlfriend's apartment. You are not to leave the premises till you hear from me. Do you understand?

SARA. Yes. *(Pause.)* I understand.

Scene 24

Sara slowly crosses the stage making a wide circle as Weber and Kersnowski exit. David enters behind her. The two of them move to the center of the stage. Sara turns to him. We are in her apartment.

DAVID. So. This is where you live.

SARA. Yes.

DAVID. Well. It's very ...

SARA. Austere.

DAVID. No.

SARA. Spartan.

DAVID. Uh, actually I was going to say ... clean. *(She laughs. A moment.)*

SARA. I'm afraid it's not much. These few rooms. My books. Papers. I keep a kind of minimalist existence.

DAVID. Well, it's nice. Uncluttered. I like it.

SARA. I've always had this idea that a person's wealth should be estimated by what she can afford to live without.

DAVID. I get it. So you must have had money at some point.

SARA. Why do you say that?

DAVID. Just a hunch.

SARA. Yes. Yes, I did. Growing up. But I'm over it now. *(Pause.)* Would you like something to drink?

DAVID. No. No, thanks. I should be, you know ... going. *(Pause.)*

SARA. I'm glad you decided to talk to me.

DAVID. Me, too.

SARA. And to walk me home. That was very ... thoughtful. I must have taken you out of your way.

DAVID. Yes. No, I mean ... it's what I wanted. To be taken out of my way, I guess.

SARA. God, all I did was talk about myself.

DAVID. I liked listening. Really. You have a lovely voice. *(She laughs.)* You do. *(Pause.)* Are you working tomorrow?

SARA. Tomorrow?

DAVID. Yeah, you said you got a job part-time at the library.

SARA. No. No, tomorrow, I can ... sleep in. *(Pause.)*

DAVID. So you'll be doing your artwork.

SARA. My what?

DAVID. Aren't you an artist of some kind? A writer?

SARA. Yes. I ... I write poems.

DAVID. Well, there you go.

SARA. But I didn't tell you that.

DAVID. No, I just ... assumed. I mean, I knew you did something smart. *(Pause.)* So you'll work on your poetry.

SARA. No. Not immediately.

DAVID. Oh. How come?

SARA. Well, I've ... uh ... it's difficult to explain.

DAVID. Try me.

SARA. Okay. I've hit a wall.

DAVID. Uh-huh.

SARA. In a manner of speaking. It's why I was out tonight. Walking. What I was doing in the park when you ... approached me.

DAVID. Right.

SARA. Working on the big picture.

DAVID. I get it.

SARA. Do you?

DAVID. Uh ... no. Not exactly. *(She smiles.)*

SARA. I used to think ... I had this idea that the reason we were put here, men and women, was to make our mark. To leave something of ourselves behind. A building. A song. A ... series of chicken scratches on broken trees. It's all over so quickly, you know?

DAVID. I know.

SARA. So. So, the point is, lately I've begun to doubt even that. I mean, here I sit, night after night, in what passes for an ivory palace, scribbling frantically in an attempt to do what? To speak to whom? I mean, my friends ... *(Pause.)* My friends are all in books. Those are the people I feel connected to. The dead ones. But — *(Pause.)*

DAVID. But where are they at two a.m. when you need someone to talk to? *(She nods.)*

SARA. Yes. *(Pause.)* I mean, what if the real labor we're supposed to be about is not some vague attempt at immortality, but rather the business of being alive? Revealing ourselves to each other? *(Pause.)* What if our lives are supposed to be our poems?

DAVID. I think I understand.

SARA. Really?

DAVID. Sure. And you were trying to write a poem ... about that. *(A moment.)*

SARA. Yes, in point of fact, I was.

DAVID. A poem about the possibility of no more poetry.

SARA. Yes.

DAVID. Well. I can see you're in a quandary, here. *(She laughs.)*

SARA. I am.

DAVID. You could read it to me.

SARA. I'm sorry?

DAVID. You could read me what you've got. I'd love to hear it.

SARA. Now?

DAVID. Is this a bad time? *(She laughs.)*

SARA. I'm not sure I know you well enough. Tell me first the most intimate details of your life.

DAVID. My life. *(Pause.)* My life is a mystery. Even to me. I've got no idea why things have fallen out the way they have. For example: You.

SARA. Me?

DAVID. How it is that I'm lucky enough to be standing here. I don't know what'll happen next. The heart beats a little faster. You smile and I wonder why.

SARA. I'm smiling because of your evasions.

DAVID. What evasions?

SARA. We were talking about *you.*

DAVID. We were? I don't recall. *(She laughs.)*

SARA. Tell me what it is you do.

DAVID. What I do. I manage a restaurant.

SARA. Oh.

DAVID. Barely manage. I own the place.

SARA. Really?

DAVID. In a manner of speaking. I'm in way over my head.

SARA. You appear to be quite successful.

DAVID. Yeah, well, that's the effect I'm going for. It's the first rule of the business. Always wear a clean shirt even though they're carving up your shoes. *(She laughs.)* I've got a favor to ask.

SARA. What's that?

DAVID. Can we get back to the big picture? *(Pause.)*

SARA. Okay.

DAVID. When I talk about my job ... when I tell you what it is I do to afford this ... rancid position that I hold down in life, the world gets small again. There's a word for it.

SARA. Myopic.

DAVID. Right. I don't want things between us to get ... myopic. I just want to forget.

SARA. Forget what?

DAVID. All of it. Everything. Right up till tonight. *(Pause.)* I'm just looking at you, see? Suddenly ideas begin to roll around in my head. I can't help myself. Everything could open up. Everything could start again. From right here. Where I'm standing. Seeing how beautiful you are.

SARA. I'm not that beautiful.

DAVID. Boy, at this moment, if you aren't, I don't know what is. *(Pause.)* I don't even know your name. *(Pause.)*

SARA. It's Sara.

DAVID. Sara. *(Pause.)* Do you know what I think, Sara?

SARA. No. Tell me.

DAVID. I think the reason people fall in love is to make themselves over from scratch. *(Pause.)* Well. It's late. I should, uh ... I should go. *(Pause.)* Shouldn't I? *(They look at each other. A moment. Then Sara moves away.)* Where are you going? *(She puts her hand on the wall. She looks at him.)* Are you going to turn out the lights?

SARA. Yes. *(And she does.)*

Scene 25

In the darkness we hear the voice of Julius Gatz.

GATZ. There is a gun aimed at you and the crack in the door. Please. Turn on the lights. *(Sara turns on the lights. David is gone. Gatz stands in the exact space that David occupied. A gun is in his hand. We are in Joyce's apartment.)* Hello.

SARA. How did you find me?

GATZ. Finding you was not hard work. I hope you don't have any plans for the evening. Sit down. *(She does.)* You've had a busy couple of days. *(Pause.)* You're much quieter than I remember.

SARA. What do you want?

GATZ. You. Amputated from my life. You've been a big time pain in the ass, lady, you know that? I don't know what you think you are. Where's the piece?

SARA. The what?

GATZ. Your weapon, Rita. Your sawed-off shotgun. Throw it on the floor.

SARA. I don't have a gun.

GATZ. Stand up. *(She does.)* Open your coat. *(She does.)* Wider. *(She does.)* What is it, in the back of your panty-hose?

SARA. I have no gun.

GATZ. You have no brains. You have no sense. You come looking for me with what? A nail file? Where'd you lose it?

SARA. I have never owned a weapon.

GATZ. I'm not laughing here.

SARA. It's the truth!

GATZ. Yeah, well, tell it to the Ice-man, Sweetcakes. If you got a through-line into hell.

SARA. Is Eisenstadt — ?

GATZ. Eisenstadt is ground beef.

SARA. What?

GATZ. Like you don't know. He bought it last night. In the alley behind his building. Two bullets through the heart. And a bunch of others all over the place. A very messy job, lady.

Very amateurish.

SARA. I didn't —

GATZ. Shut up. You went in where you don't belong. You fucked up real bad. You know what they say in my part of town?

SARA. No.

GATZ. Don't run with the big dogs if you're going to piss with the puppies. These are words to live by. I remind you of this fact albeit too late. You crazy bitch. You had your job, your looks, your nice, little apartment. And you went brain dead. For what? Love? Vengeance? A chance to prove what a man you are? I got news for you about David Ames. *(Joyce's voice is heard from offstage.)*

JOYCE. Sara?

GATZ. What? What is that?

SARA. Oh, Jesus. *(Joyce enters carrying a bag of groceries.)*

JOYCE. Sara, you left the door unlocked. *(She sees Gatz.)*

SARA. Joyce —

GATZ. You have arrived home at a very inappropriate time, Joyce. Too bad the checkout line wasn't two persons longer.

JOYCE. Who — ?

SARA. Please, don't —

GATZ. What am I going to do with you ladies? This is really a nasty place to be standing right now. But I got no choice.

SARA. Gatz, she won't —

GATZ. We're going to try to make this look like a robbery, alright? I hope I can count on your cooperation. Put the bag down, Joyce. *(Joyce does not move.)* Down. Please. *(Joyce drops the bag. She is holding a gun behind it. She fires into Gatz three times. He hits the floor.)*

SARA. Jesus Christ.

JOYCE. You heard me read him his rights, didn't you?

SARA. I ... I ...

JOYCE. Good. *(She fires into him one more time.)* Just following orders. *(She walks over to the body. She looks down at him. She turns and looks back at Sara.)* It's all over now, Sara.

Scene 26

The sound of a police siren. Marie enters as Joyce exits. Sara turns to her. The body of Gatz remains onstage through the following. We are in Marie's hotel room.

SARA. Turns out she was working for Weber the whole time.
MARIE. You're kidding me?
SARA. Undercover. He thought I needed protection. He also thought the men involved in the kidnapping might come after me. Which they did.
MARIE. Son of a bitch. And you didn't know?
SARA. Not a clue. It was a brilliant deception. But then again, it doesn't take much with me. As experience has shown.
MARIE. Don't. *(Sara shrugs.)*
SARA. What can I tell you? We grow older. We grow wiser. *(Pause.)* What will you do now?
MARIE. Go way. Get the hell out of Dodge. I got some friends down in New Orleans.
SARA. That'll be nice. *(Pause.)*
MARIE. I want to ... I want to thank you for everything you did.
SARA. No.
MARIE. You showed a lot of stuff, Sara. If I'd had that kind of strength ... who knows? Maybe David would still be alive.
SARA. Maybe *(Pause.)* But you *did* remember their names.
MARIE. Who?
SARA. Carl Eisenstadt and Julius Gatz. I mean, that took a certain kind of ... strength. Considering the hell they put you through. *(Pause.)*
MARIE. Yeah.
SARA. At first, I thought, when would they have actually used their names that night? Their full names? It seemed strange to me. But, I mean, thank God they did. And thank God you remembered. *(Pause.)*
MARIE. Yeah. Thank God.
SARA. Well. *(Pause.)* Goodbye, Marie. *(Sara holds out her hand.)*

MARIE. So long, Sara. *(Marie takes her hand.)*
SARA. Remarkable.
MARIE. What?
SARA. I was just thinking what a remarkable grip you have for someone who recently had her wrist cut open. *(A moment. Marie attempts to withdraw her hand. Sara hangs onto it. Marie pulls. Sara does not let go. Marie relaxes her arm. Sara pulls off the bandage with her free hand. She holds Marie's arm in place and stares at it. It is unblemished.)* This is some miracle cure, Marie. *(Marie pulls her hand away.)* Maybe you'd like to start at the beginning?

Scene 27

Weber enters carrying two wine glasses as Marie exits. Gatz rises and exits. Weber hands one of the glasses to Sara. We are in Sara's apartment.

SARA. What did you tell your wife?
WEBER. I was honest. I said a friend invited me over for dinner. It's not meant to be more than that, is it? *(She laughs.)*
SARA. Well, we'll see how it plays out. *(Pause.)* I ... I just wanted to find a way to show my appreciation for all you've done. Your concern. Even Joyce.
WEBER. I'm sorry about that, Sara.
SARA. Well, she did save my life. *(Sara lifts her glass.)* Cheers.
WEBER. Cheers.
SARA. To the truth. However painful. *(They touch glasses and drink.)* I have another scenario.
WEBER. What's that?
SARA. The killing of David Ames. Want to hear?
WEBER. Sure. As long as you don't mind talking about it.
SARA. On the contrary. We go back to square one. What if David was innocent of all wrong doing? What if Eisenstadt and Gatz were, indeed, partners in the Lapointe kidnapping? But their third man is not David. He is someone else. *(Pause.)* This man is sleeping with a woman named Marie Defaria. She is a cashier at a restaurant called the Fast Track. Our friend needs

his share of the money laundered. So he cuts the girl in for a percentage and she begins to do the deal. He then finds out that the police are moving faster on this than he had anticipated. They've traced the marked bills to the restaurant and are in the process of preparing to bring in the manager, one David Ames, for questioning. If they do this, David will point to Marie, and Marie will point to her boyfriend. So we have a problem. Are you with me so far?

WEBER. You've got my attention.

SARA. The obvious solution is to lose David Ames and allow the police to think that he was one of the three men responsible for the murder of Emily Lapointe and her little girl. No?

WEBER. It follows.

SARA. This man then promises Marie a larger cut if she will telephone David in the middle of the night and pretend that she has attempted to kill herself. Our friend is aware that David and Marie were once lovers. He knows that David will feel a sense of responsibility and agree to meet Marie at a local dive called Billy Hart's. David goes. He finds Marie and leaves the bar with her. And he is promptly murdered in the alley by, our friend, the other man. *(Pause.)* Good? *(A moment. Then Weber lets the mask slip from the face.)*

WEBER. Very good.

SARA. You place the body inside the dumpster. You remove the wallet. You wait by the back door of the bar and grill. When the cook comes out, having locked up for the night, you kill him. His fingerprints go on the wallet. The wallet goes in the dumpster. And the cook goes in the river. *(Pause.)* Eisenstadt and Gatz were nowhere near the bar that night. Which is why Billy Hart had to be pushed in front of a train. He would have pointed at them in court and said, "Sorry, your honor, but it was two other jokers." Two absolute strangers, in fact, who just happened to be playing pool in the bar that night. Which would have meant that Marie was lying. Which she was. She was supposed to go to that hotel room and shut up. Then one day she sees me coming up the garden path. She puts the costume bandages back on. And she starts to improvise. A story that she must have been working on for some time, actually, since her real intention was to implicate your partners. They must have known about her and she didn't like that. So she made up her mind to force your hand. Am I correct?

WEBER. Something like that. Yes.

SARA. The two of you cover up your tracks and cut your losses. Goodbye, Carl. Goodbye, Julius. A neat, little package to present to the authorities. And the problematic girlfriend asks no more questions. *(Pause.)*

WEBER. Well, Sara, you really are full of surprises.

SARA. There's just one point that remains a mystery to me.

WEBER. This I got to hear.

SARA. Why?

WEBER. Why? *(He laughs.)* Because I could. 'Cause I needed the money. No. I *wanted* the money. And the opportunity presented itself.

SARA. I take it there *was* a heroin deal.

WEBER. Correct.

SARA. Which fell apart.

WEBER. True to form.

SARA. And you found yourself with two guns pointed at both knees. A desperate man in a bad situation.

WEBER. You remember too much, Miss McKeon. It's not always the smartest way to stay alive. *(Pause.)* Someday I would love to learn how you put it all together.

SARA. No time like the present. *(Marie enters. Weber turns and sees her.)*

MARIE. Hello, Horace. *(A moment. Weber stares at her. Then he reaches into his jacket. From offstage comes the sound of another voice.)*

KERSNOWSKI. I don't think that's such a swell idea, H.E. *(Kersnowski enters with his gun casually pointed at Weber. Joyce enters behind Marie with her gun also pointed at Weber. Kersnowski crosses to Weber, removes the gun from his hand, and looks him square in the eye.)* Needless to say, I am very disappointed. *(Pause.)* Turn around, please. *(Weber does. Kersnowski pulls out a set of handcuffs and places them on Weber.)* You're under arrest for suspicion of murder. Several times over. You have the right to remain —

WEBER. Save it, Al.

KERSNOWSKI. Fine. Miss Defaria. We got a car for you downstairs.

MARIE. I'll be right there.

KERSNOWSKI. Okay. Let's go. *(Weber and Kersnowski exit. A moment.)*

SARA. You did the right thing.

MARIE. Did I? It's hard to tell. Oh, well. A reduced sentence is better than life, I guess. I mean, maybe. We'll find out.

SARA. I'd like you to leave now.

MARIE. Sure. *(Marie starts to exit. She stops.)* For what it's worth —

SARA. No —

MARIE. Having it all to do over —

SARA. Please —

MARIE. I would have chosen another way.

SARA. But there is no other way. Is there, Marie? I mean, it's done. He's dead. And now we go forward.

MARIE. Forward. Right. *(Pause.)* I remember once, we were talking, me and David, and he said he was looking for something. Something to ... turn his life around. Make him know the world in another way. Then I thought he was just making conversation. *(Pause.)* But I guess he was talking about you. *(Pause.)* Don't go *too* far forward, okay?

SARA. What do you mean? *(Marie smiles. She shakes her head. She exits followed by Joyce.)*

Scene 28

The sound of water. Sara turns and faces out as though she were watching the waves. We are on a beach. It is night. David enters. He stands at a distance, separate from her.

DAVID. The water's beautiful tonight, isn't it? *(She turns and sees him. She looks back at the water. A moment.)*

SARA. Yes.

DAVID. The way it comes in slow then dive bombs into the

rocks. Violent. Tough. But it's a pussycat, really. Gentle as can be. *(Pause.)* I love the sound of it. That steady rhythm. Like a low hum, then: Whoosh! Crack! Down it comes. Away it goes back out into the ... what? The unknown, I guess. *(Pause.)* You're very quiet. That's a nice quality. Still waters run deep, no? You've got a kind of intelligence there. It registers right away. Really. Even from a distance. It's like a ... a light. A beacon. Truly. Some people would have no business standing along a landscape this way. They'd ruin it. But you. You fit right in. *(Pause.)*

SARA. Do I know you?

DAVID. Not at present. But you could. With very little effort. I could make myself known to you. I could tell you the story of my life. I would rather hear the story of your life, because, frankly, mine is like a bad movie I've seen too many times.

SARA. Are you high on something?

DAVID. Nope.

SARA. Drunk? *(He shrugs.)*

DAVID. I've been drinking, but I'm not ripped by any stretch. I'm just ... feeling good. At peace with myself. My surroundings. The world at large. I like standing here. Doing nothing. Talking to you. *(Pause.)* Listen, I know I sound like an idiot. Some transient con-artist who's cornered you along the rocks. Such is not the case. I've just been admiring you. Your poise. You've got a kind of dignity there. It's the rare occurrence. I only wanted to pay the compliment. *(Pause.)* So what do you think of me so far?

SARA. I have to go.

DAVID. I understand. It's embarrassing when someone speaks how it is they feel. From the heart, as it were. Who knows? I could be dangerous. You have to decide. Do I keep talking to him? Do I keep letting him talk to me? If I stand here much longer I might give off the impression I'm the kind of woman who likes getting picked up in the park. If this were a pick-up.

SARA. Isn't it?

DAVID. Could be. I honestly hadn't thought that far ahead. *(Pause.)*

64

SARA. I really do have to go.

DAVID. Of course. To continue any further would be to encourage me. All the same. It might have been nice. I'd have been nice to you. I know that sounds like a line, but it's not. I've never said that to anyone before. Look. *(Pause.)* Look, all I meant to imply was that I could stand a friend. How about you? You ever run out of friends? *(Pause.)* I guess not.

SARA. I —

DAVID. No, it's okay. I took a chance, is all. *(Pause.)*

SARA. Well. *(Pause.)* Well, it was very nice to meet you. Thanks for the, uh ... compliment.

DAVID. Sure. Anytime. *(She turns and walks to the edge of the stage. David remains looking out at the water. A moment. Then she turns back. She looks at him.)*

SARA. Could — ?

DAVID. Yes? *(Pause.)*

SARA. Could we just stand here for a moment?

DAVID. Sure. I'm not going anywhere. *(She looks out at the water. He does the same. She turns and looks at him. He looks at her. They stand this way. Looking at each other. The sound of the water continues.)*

End of Play

PROPERTY PLOT

Styrofoam cup (Kersnowski)
Telephone (Preset)
Payphone (Preset)
Cigarettes (Weber)
Lighter (Weber)
Notepad (Kersnowski)
Pencil (Kersnowski)
Wrapped bagel (Kersnowski)
Book (Preset)
Stack of books (Joyce)
File (Weber)
Doughnut (Kersnowski)
2 coffee cups (Joyce)
Bartender's tray (Billy)
Large glass with ice (Billy)
Small glass with ice (Billy)
Scotch bottle (Billy)
Drambuie bottle (Billy)
Bar towel (Billy)
2 menus (Weber)
1/2 candy bar (Kersnowski)
Ledger book (David)
Pen (David)
Book of Dylan Thomas poems (David)
Beer bottle (Weber)
Program (Eisenstadt)
Set of keys (Preset)
Handgun (Weber)
Handgun (Kersnowski)
Shot glass (Billy)
Up glass (Billy)
Whiskey bottle (Billy)
Tray (Gatz)
Plate of food (Gatz)
Knife (Gatz)

Fork (Gatz)
Napkin (Gatz)
Small black datebook (Gatz)
Cigarettes (Gatz)
Lighter (Gatz)
Handgun (Gatz)
Bag of groceries (Joyce)
Handgun (Joyce)
Blanks (Joyce)
2 wine glasses (Weber)
Pair of handcuffs (Kersnowski)

COSTUME PLOT

Scene 1
  Sara: Man's shirt and undergarments
  David: Double-breasted suit, dress shirt and tie

Scene 2
  Kersnowski: Suit, shirt and tie
  Weber: Suit, shirt and tie

Scene 3
  Sara: Summer dress
  Weber: Same as above
  Kersnowski: Same as above

Scene 4
  Sara: Same as above
  Joyce: Blouse and slacks

Scene 5
  Sara: Same as above
  David: Double-breasted suit, dress shirt and tie

Scene 6
  Sara: Same as above
  Weber: Suit pants, shirt, tie and shoulder holster
  Kersnowski: Suit pants, shirt, tie and shoulder holster

Scene 7
  Sara: Same as above
  Joyce: Blouse and slacks

Scene 8
  Sara: Add summer jacket
  Billy: Short-sleeved shirt and jeans

Scene 9
    Sara: Same as above
    Weber: Suit, shirt and tie

Scene 10
    Sara: Same as above
    Kersnowski: Suit, shirt and tie

Scene 11
    Sara: Lose jacket
    David: Suit pants, dress shirt and tie

Scene 12
    Sara: Same as above
    Weber: Suit, shirt and tie
    Eisenstadt: Suit, shirt and bow tie

Scene 13
    Sara: Same as above
    Eisenstadt: Same as above

Scene 14
    Sara: Add jacket
    Eisenstadt: Same as above

Scene 15
    Sara: Lose jacket
    David: Suit pants, dress shirt and tie

Scene 16
    Sara: Same as above
    Weber: Suit, shirt and tie
    Kersnowski: Suit, shirt and tie

Scene 17
    Sara: Add jacket
    Billy: Short-sleeved shirt and jeans

Scene 18
    Sara: Same as above
    Marie: Kimono, undergarments and bandages

Scene 19
    Sara: Same as above
    Gatz: Suit, open shirt and jewelry

Scene 20
    Sara: Same as above
    Joyce: Running clothes

Scene 21
    Sara: Same as above
    Billy: Rib t-shirt and jeans

Scene 22
    Sara: Same as above
    Marie: Kimono, undergarments and bandages

Scene 23
    Sara: Same as above
    Weber: Suit pants, shirt, tie and shoulder holster
    Kersnowski: Suit pants, shirt, tie and shoulder holster

Scene 24
    Sara: Same as above
    David: Double-breasted suit, dress shirt and tie

Scene 25
    Sara: Same as above
    Gatz: Suit, open shirt and jewelry
    Joyce: Running clothes

Scene 26
    Sara: Same as above
    Marie: Blouse, tight jeans and bandages

Sceme 27
    Sara: Lose jacket (but add near end of scene)
    Weber: Suit, shirt and tie
    Kersnowski: Suit, shirt and tie
    Marie: Blouse and tight jeans
    Joyce: Blouse and slacks

Scene 28
    Sara: Same as above
    David: Double-breasted suit, dress shirt and tie

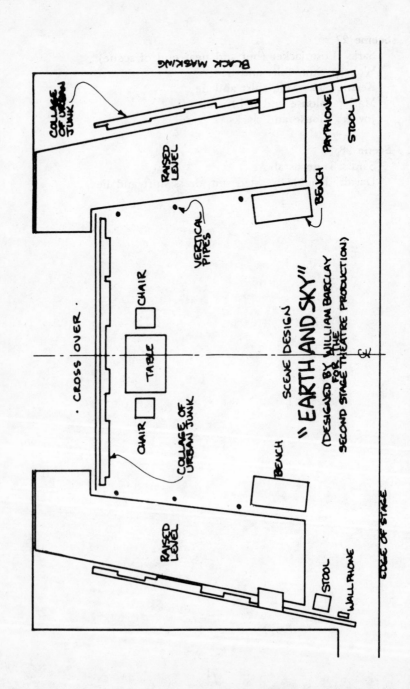

SCENE DESIGN

"EARTH AND SKY"

(DESIGNED BY WILLIAM BARCLAY FOR THE
SECOND STAGE THEATRE PRODUCTION)

NEW PLAYS

THE GRAPES OF WRATH
by Frank Galati

THE AMERICAN PLAN
by Richard Greenberg

LIFE DURING WARTIME
by Keith Reddin

MOUNTAIN LANGUAGE
by Harold Pinter

SPUNK
by George C. Wolfe

ABUNDANCE
by Beth Henley

Write for information as to availability

DRAMATISTS PLAY SERVICE, INC.
440 Park Avenue South   New York, N.Y. 10016

NEW PLAYS

BEFORE IT HITS HOME
by Cheryl L. West

APPROXIMATING MOTHER
by Kathleen Tolan

THE MANCHURIAN CANDIDATE
by John Lahr

VEINS AND THUMBTACKS
by Jonathan Marc Sherman

BARGAINS
by Jack Heifner

ARTIFICIAL REALITY
by Jeffrey Essmann

Write for information as to availability

DRAMATISTS PLAY SERVICE, INC.
440 Park Avenue South   New York, N.Y. 10016

NEW PLAYS

FOUR BABOONS ADORING THE SUN
by John Guare

THE KATHY AND MO SHOW: PARALLEL LIVES
by Mo Gaffney and Kathy Najimy

RAFT OF THE MEDUSA
by Joe Pintauro

STATES OF SHOCK
by Sam Shepard

MINOR DEMONS
by Bruce Graham

DEARLY DEPARTED
by David Bottrell and Jessie Jones

Write for information as to availability

DRAMATISTS PLAY SERVICE, INC.
440 Park Avenue South   New York, N.Y. 10016

NEW PLAYS

I HATE HAMLET
by Paul Rudnick

THE OLD BOY
by A.R. Gurney

THE FEVER
by Wallace Shawn

DAYTRIPS
by Jo Carson

LA BÊTE
by David Hirson

FORTINBRAS
by Lee Blessing

Write for information as to availability

DRAMATISTS PLAY SERVICE, INC.
440 Park Avenue South   New York, N.Y. 10016

NEW PLAYS

SIX DEGREES OF SEPARATION
by John Guare

BREAKING LEGS
by Tom Dulack

SEARCH AND DESTROY
by Howard Korder

THE SNOW BALL
by A.R. Gurney

BEGGARS IN THE HOUSE OF PLENTY
by John Patrick Shanley

DISTANT FIRES
by Kevin Heelan

Write for information as to availability

DRAMATISTS PLAY SERVICE, INC.
440 Park Avenue South   New York, N.Y. 10016